Understand and Complete The 12 Steps Of Alcoholics Anonymous

Your Guide to All 12 Steps

An Easy To Follow Guide in Today's Language

by Anonymous Guest

"**Understand and Complete One Step At A Time in Alcoholics Anonymous**" Selected, Compiled & Edited by: Anonymous Guest 2013 Copyright © May 2013 by Anonymous Guest All rights reserved. No part of this book may be used or reproduced in any manner whatsoever without the express written permission of the publisher except for the use of brief quotations in a book review.

ISBN-13: 978-1521921326

ISBN-10: 1521921326

ISBN Canada: 978-0-9951679-2-6

Table of Contents

Introduction 1
Step 1 4
Step 2 16
Step 3 28
Step 4 38
Step 5 56
Step 6 65
Step 7 68
Step 8 70
Step 9 73
Step 10 79
Step 11 85
Step 12 91

Recommended Books 97

Dedication

I dedicate this book to my first sponsor Blair T. A truly amazing man who took me through my first set of 12 steps and showed me the way to

"The Great Spirit".

I will be forever grateful.

Introduction

What I am doing is offering a guide to each Step from the Big Book of Alcoholics Anonymous. This guide is not intended to replace the Big Book in any way, it is simply offered as additional help as you go through your steps. It's not unusual to hear at a meeting that a person is having a problem with one or more steps out of the Big Book.

So I have written a guide in today's language that may help explain to you more of what each step is about and how it works. I recommend having your Big Book with you as you use this guide. If you do not have a Big Book with you but have access to the internet, you can read an online version which is available to read free in English, French or Spanish. Go to this URL:

http://www.aa.org/bigbookonline/

With over 38 years' experience in Alcoholics Anonymous, thousands of hours in Big Book studies and years of sponsoring dozens of people, I wanted to leave my strength, hope, and experience to those who may not be able to get to meetings as often as they would like. I've been mentored by incredible people who showed me the principals, promises, and keys to sobriety within the pages of the Big Book.

I've met people from small towns that had only one meeting a week, others who were working on cruise liners, and some in the hospitals and in jails who just don't have access to all the AA has to offer. In situations and environments like these it can take hundreds of meetings to see the working solution that is offered through the 12 Steps. This book is offered in the hopes to make that process of understanding what the steps have to offer somewhat easier.

This is why the newcomer is the most important person in the meeting when they arrive. It is not so they can help fill the ranks when the old timers pass away. Not at all.

The **only** reason the new comer is the most important person in the room is because that meeting they go to may be the only opportunity they will ever have to hear the message of hope that will inspire them to get started in the Recovery Program known as the 12 Steps of AA.

Many times we go to a meeting and hear more about how people used to drink than the solution they found to stay sober. So I want to share this message of recovery with you, like it was done for me. All that I ask is that you use the Big Book as your reference. Highlight your book with what you learn here and make the Big Book your own study and recovery book, then, pass on what you learn.

Fair enough?

What I have done is put together a guide through each individual step to help you along the way. Keep in mind that no single individual speaks for Alcoholics Anonymous. The Big Book itself contains the full prescription to a happy and sober life. The interpretation of that book sometimes causes some confusion because in was written in the language of 1939 but with the help of a good AA sponsor, a few Big Book Studies, and talking to your Higher Power on a regular basis, it will become clear.

The funny thing is once you see it, the simplicity will almost make you laugh. Perhaps you've heard it before: "I can't, He can, and now I'll let Him". It falls in line with "HOW" it Works. "Honesty, Open mindedness, and Willingness".

This is the roadmap to discovery (one step at a time) in what will prove to be a life changing journey for you in Alcoholics Anonymous. If you chose to use it.

Let's get started.

Proceeds from this book will be donated back to Alcoholics Anonymous and its supporting organizations.

Step One

"We admitted we were powerless over alcohol and that our lives had become unmanageable."

I want to point out the importance of seeing this step as two distinct statements. First that we are powerless over alcohol, **and** that our lives had become unmanageable. Let's start with the first part of this sentence:

We admitted we were powerless over alcohol.

When I first joined AA over 38 years ago it was pretty easy to admit I was powerless over alcohol because of my behavior while drinking. I still had some reservations because I didn't get in trouble every time I drank but when I did, it could get pretty bad. So I conceded to this statement in that context. However, as the years went by, and I watched newcomers and even some old-timers go back to drinking, I saw and understood the truth behind this powerful warning.

It meant I was powerless over alcohol even after all these years sober! After any period of sobriety, I was still powerless from taking that drink again. It did not matter how many days, months, or years I had accumulated, I was powerless to stop myself from drinking alcohol on a permanent basis. Matter of fact, that's exactly how my first sponsor put the first step to me. We went to his home the night after he became my sponsor and sat me down at his kitchen table.

He looked me square in the face and said "You need to understand that one day you will drink again and there is nothing you can do about it"! You could have knocked me over with a feather when he laid it on me like that!

After a minute of my standing there with my mouth open he smiled and said "But there is a solution". He had achieved in a few seconds what AA meetings had not yet achieved over the last 4 years. I had begun to really understand the true nature of this disease.

Let's consider how the Big Book gets this point across

More About Alcoholism

Chapter 3 (pg. 30) of the Second Edition Alcoholics Anonymous

This chapter in the Big Book is dedicated to Step One exclusively. The importance of understanding the dilemma we are in and why. Without full knowledge of what we have, how can we understand what is needed to effectively deal with it?

I've heard it said in meetings that you don't have to admit you're an alcoholic to do the steps. That is incorrect. Right at the start of the chapter it is stressed to us that "we have to concede (give in and stop fighting) to our innermost selves that we were alcoholics. This is the first step in recovery."

Deep inside us is a desire to drink freely like other people. It's our release, the way to breathe again. However for us it's also the way to ruin. We can't guarantee that the next time it will be different when we drink. There is no promise of control. Not over just our drinking, but also over our behavior.

We must remember that what defines us as a carrier of alcoholism is that we show the symptoms of the disease both drinking, **and** while we are sober.

While drinking we have the Dr. Jekyll Mr. Hyde syndrome of two personalities. Our perception of reality changes once we have a few drinks. Yet, everyone is different. Some may feel more relaxed and their sense of nervousness disappears (that was mine) or we become belligerent and easily argumentative. These are only a couple examples, there are hundreds of personality types alcoholics display when they drink but this gives you an idea of what I'm saying.

The Big Book says the natural state of a (sober) alcoholic is irritable, restless and discontent, unless they can again experience the sense of ease and relief that comes with a few drinks.

The key here is to realize we are not like other people. Not just as drinkers but as sober individuals. We have a deep malady or sickness that affects the deepest part of us, our spirit.

The book openly states that we are not like other people, it is a delusion and we have to reject (or smash) this self-imposed delusion now. We are different and **always** will be.

But all is not lost. This will become a huge advantage to us when we come to Step 3 and get the Force of the Universe behind us. It's a life changing Power that will not only change our lives but also those who are put in our path. It will become the Joy of your life, just wait and see.

But I'm getting a little ahead of myself. Let's stay on course. Seeing that we have this disease even though we are not drinking, this disease will continue to worsen while we are sober. This fact will reveal itself in two ways.

One, while we are sober we can become more and more irritable as time goes by. Little things anger us and we can overreact to seemingly small situations. We're not happy no matter what we get or achieve. Something important is missing. We just don't know what it is, yet.

Second, if we return to drinking we will be as bad as ever "in a short period of time." This is the critical point. It may not be bad right away. It might even be fine for a while, but in a short period of time we find ourselves drinking and behaving in the same manner (or worse) than before.

Then it hits the fan.

If you are observant and go to enough meetings you will meet those who tried going back to drinking. Listen to their experience. Almost all of them all agree that their drinking was worse after their period of sobriety, in a short period of time.

Hopefully you won't need to learn that lesson first hand, but if you do, I hope you survive and make it back to warn others. Unfortunately, many don't make it back and we bury good people who didn't understand the "nature" of their condition.

Please don't be one of them. It's not necessary because there **is** an answer that works.

The case in point the Big Book shows as examples are 2 individuals for us to consider. Jim and Fred.

Here's Jim's story in a nutshell:

He owned an automobile agency, was a good salesman and a war veteran. He was intelligent and appeared normal "so far as we can see, except for a nervous disposition".

He didn't start drinking until he was 35 but in a short period of time, he became violent when drinking. That was his "Mr. Hyde", having a different personality when he drank. (It can be subtle or obvious to others around us). He wound up in a mental asylum and met up with some members of Alcoholics Anonymous.

They explained the disease of alcoholism and the solution they found and he joined AA. His drinking had caused him to lose his automobile agency and he was now working there as a salesman.

In rapid succession he went through multiple drunken episodes but he couldn't stop. So they asked him to go over what happened prior to his drinking bouts.

Here are the key points;

He was **irritated** that he was now working for a place he used to own. He even had an argument with the boss (but nothing serious).

He *felt hungry* and stopped at a roadside bar to get some food *and had no intention or thought of drinking.* He had been there many times in the past.

Then he had a brainstorm. The dumb idea that if he put an ounce of whiskey in his milk after he finished eating it couldn't hurt him. He had a vague sense that what he was doing was stupid but felt reassured that a full stomach would protect him.

The experiment went so well he had another, and another, and another...

The next sentence tells us what happened: "Thus started one more journey to the asylum for Jim."

Remember Jim's an intelligent person, but his normal reasoning or "sanity" was easily pushed aside for this dumb idea of mixing it with milk! He realized that sound reasoning will not work. Especially when we are **hungry, angry, lonely, or tired**. (ever hear this phrase?)

Cool, let's look at our next example, Fred.

Fred is a partner in a big accounting firm, has a great home, been married for a number of years with grown up kids. Almost like a perfect home.

His personality is very outgoing and gets along with almost everyone because of it. He is the type of person (it seems) everyone would like to be. Yet his drinking put him in the hospital.

While meeting with a couple AA members he told them that he was there to "rest his nerves" even though the doctor had told him otherwise. The AA members told him of the **spiritual remedy** for his condition but he did not believe himself to be an alcoholic. He admitted to having the symptoms of alcoholism but not that he was powerless to do anything about it.

Nothing was heard about Fred for a while. Then one day they heard he was back in the hospital. They did not go to see him however until **he** indicated he wanted to see them. This is the principal of attraction rather than promotion. We must let people want help or else we may prevent them from hitting the bottom they need to get serious.

Fred told them his story but it was a little different from Jim's experience.

Here is Fred's story:

For a while he was content and confident while staying sober and one day was out of town for a government contract. The key elements of this particular day were; He **felt fine, no pressing problems or worries**. He had landed a great contract and knew his partners would be happy about it **so he was happy**. He even went as far to say "**It was the end of a perfect day, not a cloud on the horizon**".

Then, the **brainstorm**. The insane reason that came to mind that said he could drink again. And he did!

He later told them that not only had he been off guard, but he didn't even resist the first drink. He drank without any concern at all for what could happen.

Then he recalled how they told him in his first meeting with them that *if* he had an alcoholic mind he *would* drink again. Even though he would have a good defense system, it would fall away for some trivial reason why he could drink again, and it did.

Then they outlined the spiritual program of action for him to follow which was working for hundreds of others.

Now, let's step back and look at these two examples.

Jim was **hungry** before he drank, **angry** because he had an argument with his boss. Then was **alone** and got struck with a crazy idea he could drink on a stomach with milk in it.

Sort of the hungry, angry, lonely, tired phrase you may have heard.

Then there's Fred.

He was happy. He landed a big contract and knew he was going to be the star of the show landing a big Government contract. He even said his future looked bright!

So, this would be happy, joyous and even had a bright future. But he got drunk too!

That is why this chapter says the alcoholic has no *effective* mental defense against the first drink. We are cursed with this insanity that will cripple our defenses eventually and bring us back to drinking. It's just a matter of time.

It wisely says "at certain times" we will have no effective defense because for a while you might have a good defense. Maybe the loss of your job or your family. Or even your freedom if you should drink again. But if you have the disease of alcoholism you are doomed to drink again.

The only (proven) effective defense has to come from a Higher Power. It promises (on page 42) that spiritual solutions would solve **all** our problems. This is a huge promise. Hold on to this one, it has been a key to my own problems throughout my sobriety. Anytime I found myself in a jackpot I remembered that promise and always found a way out with my Higher Power.

The final premise this book makes in this chapter is that if you are alcoholic, you will drink again. There is no *human power* that can prevent it. However, a Higher Power **can** and **will** if you let it.

Before I end this part of the chapter, I want to cover the second part of Step One. That our lives had become unmanageable.

The reason why our lives are unmanageable is because we suffer from extreme self-centeredness and it impairs our ability to properly manage our affairs. However, once we decide to invite a Higher Power into our lives this will no longer become an issue.

On page 62 in chapter 5 (How it Works) you will find the phrase: "the alcoholic is an extreme example of self will run riot". Above everything we alcoholics must be rid of this selfishness. We must or it kills us! God makes that possible".

We can decide to let this Higher Power to be in charge of the outcome of our daily actions. We will do the work and He will steer the boat (so to speak) to its intended course.

The word "manage" is the key to understanding the statement. Consider this:

A manager is responsible for the *outcome* of the effort of those he is in charge of. But with us, because we have extreme self-centeredness, our desire is to have our actions or efforts give a certain result.

Example;

You open a door for a lady it would be nice if she say thanks. If they say "you sexist pig", you're angry. (this actually happened to friend of mine) However if your intent was only to be kind, the outcome is really none of your business. Whether they say thanks, or whatever, it doesn't matter. Your job is the action, not the result. Get it?

So now we give up trying to manage our actions by doing what we need to do but leave the results or final outcome up to our Higher Power.

It's a spiritual principal that will set you free for good. Not only that, it will give you the peace you sought in the bottle. It won't be an easy thing to learn but once you do, it's a life changer!

We even made a slogan about it: "Let Go and Let God"

Next, I'll reveal the discovery found in Step 2 that will make it an easy step to do, and understand.

Step Two

Step 2 is covered in chapter 4 "**We Agnostics**"

"Came to believe that a Power greater than ourselves could restore us to sanity".

I think the first time I looked at this step I felt the same way as most people do. What the heck is sanity?

I don't know if I've ever had a sane day in my life. Sure, I've had lots of great days, wonderful memories, but most wound up in bad experiences. Somewhere I screwed things up. I didn't have a bad experience every time things were going well but I guess it's safe to say I had more bad experiences than good.

When reading the Big Book my sponsor gave me a great tip: Never assume I understand a particular word. Look it up in the dictionary. If I don't find a definition that speaks to me in that dictionary, find another dictionary. When I find a definition that describes or defines that word in the way I need to understand it, it will resonate with me.

Just that one tip has contributed to my sobriety in a huge way, so I suggest you do the same. Don't assume, look it up. When you find a good definition for you, you'll know. It has become something that I still enjoy doing.

When it came to the word "sanity", I went searching for a definition I could understand because I couldn't make any sense of that word. I had nothing to refer to!

I think it was the second or third dictionary I found that gave me a definition that meant something to me. This is what it said:

"Sanity can be seen in terms of balance."

Balance! That I can understand. It was easy to see areas of my life that had no balance. My finances, my work, relationships, money, the list went on and on. It seemed my whole life was out of balance. But this step said that a Power greater than myself could bring sanity [or balance] into my life. When I considered it that way, I actually got excited!

Not only that, I discovered that it actually promised I would develop a BELIEF that my Higher Power would bring balance to ALL areas of my life.

Let's take a look at some important parts of Step 2 that are covered in Chapter 4.

You'll see at the bottom of page 44 (We Agnostics) a critical point about self-reliance and our behaviors as alcoholics.

"If a mere code of morals or a better philosophy of life was sufficient to overcome alcoholism, many of us would have recovered long ago".

I think this is the only time the Big Book ever got me mad. I don't know where the anger came from, but it was telling me I cannot manage my way into sobriety.

It was telling me that I could try to be the nice person, stop lying, stop stealing, stop preying on other people, it didn't matter. I was screwed. I can try to be the good person all I wanted, I have a disease and it's in charge. Changing my attitude is not going to change my alcoholism.

Another way to look at it that helps me to better understand it, is to compare it to another disease. I have diabetes. Changing my attitude or appearance isn't going to affect my diabetes at all. I can wash my face, comb my hair, even dress better but it won't matter. Diabetes is still there and I will still have an attack if I don't follow a simple method of recovery one day at a time.

I think it made me angry because I wanted to be in control. I don't want to work hard, I don't want to get honest. I didn't want to give up anything. It's easier for me to just be lazy. But I can't afford that when it comes alcoholism. Because alcoholism continues to affect me whether I'm drinking or not.

In the Chapter called The Doctor's Opinion, you'll find the following statement.

"They are restless, irritable and discontented, unless they can again experience the sense of ease and comfort which comes at once by taking a few drinks"

When we are sober, we lose our sanity, little by little. Over time I will become restless, irritable and discontented until I can get a few drinks in me. Then I'm at peace again.

The longer I was *without* a drink (to take the edge off) the easier it was to irritate me. Just ask anyone who hung around me. Especially my past girlfriends.

Going back to the step, it says we need to find a Power that can do for us what we can't do for ourselves. To have real balance in our lives. In everything!

This means not only with our drinking problem but with our sober problem! I don't know about you but I couldn't stay drunk and I couldn't stay sober. I couldn't pay my bills and I couldn't keep a job. I hurt the people closest to me in spite of not wanting to. I just kept moving from one jackpot to another. So the idea that I could rid my life of these issues was a pretty cool idea and I was ready for it.

Perhaps at this point you're not impressed, maybe you don't believe in a God of the universe, Creator of all things.

Well I've got good news for you. You don't have to!

All you have to do is find a WILLINGNESS to believe that there is something out there that can help you. Actually, this is the main purpose of the Big Book. If you do some research, you'll find on page 20 and page 45 that it says it's the main purpose of this book to help you find a Power by which you can live.

With just a *willingness to believe* that there is something out there and is capable of helping you is all you need to get started. That's it, that's all. You don't have to define it, give it a name, or anything else. Just start with that willingness.

I'm going to tell you a little bit of my story at this point because some people have had the same issue I had.

I had some bad experiences with religious people and religious organizations when I was young. The type of situations most people never talk about. I just want to tell you, if you've had the same abusive past, you can still do this. I know because it worked for me and many others who had my same past experiences and worse.

This is a spiritual program, not a religious one.

A religious program is something that says you must do this and you must do that. If you don't follow the rules, you're out.

With spirituality there are no rules. We only seek.

At most meetings you'll hear them read:

"We are not saints. The point is, that we are willing to grow along spiritual lines. The principles we have set down our guides to progress. We claim spiritual progress rather than spiritual perfection."

We are on a whole new path now, a spiritual path. A spiritual path that we can be on together, one step at a time.

At this point I'm going to give you a gift. One that was given to me and it changed my life and brought me to where I am today. I'm going to show you the road I was shown that brought me to discovering a Higher Power.

This will work for you, all you need is the willingness.

What I want you to do, is take out a piece of paper and write down 4 things you would want from a Higher Power. The characteristics you would need Him (or Her or It) to have so you could trust it.

Some of us have had issues with our parents, so placing our trust in a male figure, or even a female figure has been a problem, maybe for a long time now. But this has nothing at all to do with that and it is important we make that clear.

If you have had problems in the past in this area, I'm going to ask you not to relate it to what we are doing. Besides you're going to create your Higher Power in a way that works for you. This will correct it.

With this piece of paper you will list 4 things that you will need from a Higher Power so you can rely on Him.

If you need a little help here, I can offer some suggestions.

What I did is I gave Him characteristics I needed so I could know the needed power was there.

First, was that He would love me in spite of myself. I had a bad habit of screwing up every relationship I ever had.

Two, He would have the necessary power to get things done. No matter what it was, He was capable of getting it fixed.

Three, he would be the Father I never had. He would always be there, no matter what. He would never abandon me, die, or be too busy.

(My own father died as a result of his drinking. His drinking broke up our family when I was a child. I met him again when I was eighteen, and then two or three times again over the next fifteen years until he passed.)

We never talked about anything important, just "how you doing" and "what's new" kind of stuff. Anytime I asked him to explain what happened, just so I could understand, he would pass it off and say that we could talk about it later.

Unfortunately, later never came, and I buried a stranger.

That's why I considered a father figure to be important. Deep inside I wanted one I could look up to, so I needed this new Father to be more than mine was.

When it came time to figure out the fourth characteristic of my Higher Power it was a little more difficult. It took me about two or three days to find the fourth characteristic I wanted. Funny thing was, I was not alone! Ninety percent of the people I've suggested this to, have had the same problem.

If this happens with you, just let it go. Give it a couple of days and see what comes to mind. It may happen when you're waking up in the morning, or just before you go to sleep. But you'll get an inspiration on the final characteristic that you want.

You can use some of mine if you need to, just make sure that these are characteristics *you* need.

Let's look at some others.

Someone who is honest, trustworthy, loving, no matter what, all-powerful, can't be injured, will never die, will never leave us, and will never be at a loss for what to do.

No threatening characteristics though! None. Nothing like: will cause bad things to happen or not allow good things to work out for me or send me to hell if I mess up. Only good characteristics. This is very important!

So many of us have had strict disciplinarians in our life and maybe we even grew up thinking this was a good thing. I'm not looking to start a debate in this area, I'm just asking you NOT to add anything like this to your list, ok?

Awesome.

Once you have this piece of paper with your four characteristics, I want you to keep it in your Big Book. You can even staple it to a page so you don't lose it.

For now, this will be who your Higher Power is. Nothing else! That is very important. You need a Higher Power you can trust and rely on, so only use this to start from. I promise you; this will work like gangbusters!

I can honestly say everything that has happened to me since I started this over 38 years ago, everything has worked out for my good. Every single time. No exceptions.

I've even had a good friend of mine who is a Pastor and runs a men's retreat ask to use this process at his retreat. A number of men have great difficulty in this area (accepting a Higher Power) and it takes a lot of stress off the problem. I'm sure the same problem happens with our lady members as well.

I'll give you the last characteristic I used when I did this list for the first time. It was a little difficult for me but because of my past but I knew I needed to add this point to the list.

The final characteristic I chose for my Higher Power was that He would do what was right for me even if I didn't agree with it.

That one was a little scary for me but I knew it was necessary. All or most of the decisions I have made in the past were wrong. They brought me to a bottom I don't ever want to see again.

In case you already believe in God, I suggest you still do this process. If you want to add more than four characteristics to the list that's fine, but no more than six to start. Again, no scary or threatening characteristics. You won't need them. You'll understand why later.

Simplicity is the key, and later on this list will be expanded, all by itself in Step 11.

Don't worry if you're concerned that the God of your present understanding may be offended by this. I guarantee you He is not. God doesn't have an ego. He won't be offended in the least. Later on, you'll actually find your relationship with Him will improve greatly.

Congratulations, you now have a Higher Power! And you don't have to defend Him to anyone! The "came to believe" part will happen soon enough. You have now landed on the path, with both feet. This is the simplicity of the program. One step at a time, just for today. Nothing is forced.

Just as a suggestion, I recommend you keep the specifics of this guide and what you are doing, to yourself. Feel free to tell people that you're working on the steps but don't try to explain the process until you fully understand it. Even though what we are doing it right out of the Big Book.

The reason for this is because some people may try to discourage you from your path. They may even come up with some logical reason why you should not use a guide with the Big Book of Alcoholics Anonymous.

Even when I was in a Big Book study with my sponsor, he suggested the same thing. To refrain from trying to explain what we are doing with the Big Book in our study to others. We were only using the Big Book at the time but we were just beginning to understand what it really meant. How each step translated into our lives and the keys of life that were held within that book.

Feel free however to discuss it with your sponsor, if you have one. I'm simply suggesting to keep it simple. Don't open yourself to possible discouragement. Once this process begins to work for you people will see the enthusiasm in your face. Then once you understand the process fully, you can share it from the Big Book because you will "truly" know how it works (pun intended).

I do not suggest that you use any organization as a Higher Power. This is because organizations are "human" based. And people let people down. Even using your own group as your Higher Power can lead to a fall.

Many new groups have been created as a result of resentment due to someone in your home group. Maybe from a business meeting. You certainly don't want to place your sobriety in the hands of erstwhile erratic alcoholics. Well-meaning as we are, we can still hurt people.

So let's keep this step a spiritual one. Remember that you don't "have to" believe, only be "willing" to believe. That's all you need to get started and to affect a real contact with a Higher Power.

In Step 3 I'll reveal some very special discoveries to this step that will make your sobriety the easiest thing you do!

Step Three

Step 3 is in Chapter 5 "**How it Works**"

"**Made the decision to turn our will and our lives over to the care of God as we understood him.**"

The first part of this chapter is read at most AA meetings. You'll recognize this chapter with the opening phrase "**Rarely have we seen a person fail who has thoroughly followed our path.**"

I'll share with you just how screwed up I was when I first came to AA. When they read that sentence my mind told me they were talking about me. I would be the rare case that would thoroughly follow the path but still fail. So there was no point in me trying. That's how bad my mind was. It was like it was out to get me.

I still remember that sinking feeling when I heard my mind say that to me. Thankfully I found a good sponsor later and he told me I didn't have to believe those voices. Wow, I never considered that. I thought those voices were real and speaking the truth. That was a relief!

Now there are a lot of really important points in this chapter. I'm going to ask for your patience as I cover them one by one. Then at the end of this, I'll bring it all together.

One of the points it gives is that those who **do not** recover are people who cannot or will not *completely* [surrender] give themselves to this simple program.

This means to give up the fight. To stop trying to do it your way and surrendered to an effective way to get sober.

It's also important that you are personally convinced you can't do it on your own. Maybe you're coming into your first AA meeting and you've got some sobriety time behind you. Maybe a few days, a few months, or even a few years.

I met a man in Edmonton Alberta who came to his first meeting after twenty-years without a drink. He was in the back yard mowing his lawn when his daughter came up to him and gave him the cash to buy a case of beer. She told him at least when he was drunk they could put up with him. But since he had been sober, he was been a consistent pain in the ass.

Remember what I said earlier about the natural state of an alcoholic sober being irritable, restless, and discontented?

He came into the meeting with 20 years without a drink and realized it wasn't enough, he still could lose his family. He started the recovery process and his family is still together today *and* they're happy.

With me, I was scared to death of my anger. It was like a switch inside of me that I lived in fear of. If the switch got turned on, I couldn't turn it off. In that state I was as uncontrollable just like when I drank, maybe even worse. I lived in fear of that anger until I went through the 12 steps.

If you stick around long enough, you're going to see people come into the meetings and then go back out to try it again. It seems like a very small percentage of those people ever make it back. It's just not a gamble I'm prepared to take, and thankfully don't have to. I hope you don't take that chance either.

The first part of this step says "made a decision,"

It's important that the decision be made before doing this step. The question it is asking is, how you doing so far? Have you been sober a little while? Are you happy with your progress so far? Do you want to stop trying to stay sober *your* way? Are you ready to concede that you need help from a Power greater than yourself to have successful *happy* sobriety?

If you're not ready to make this decision, don't do it yet. However, if you are, you're in store for some great news. That news is that your sobriety is now going to be placed in the hands of your Higher Power. He will be in charge of that area of your life from now on.

This is what it means when we turn over our will and our life to the care of God as we (now) understand

Him. I'm speaking about the Higher Power you created in Step Two with that piece of paper I suggested.

Our will is what we want for ourselves. We want to be sober and we want to be happy. We want to be able to have money to support ourselves and maybe have our families back, but we just can't be consistent in doing what is needed to keep these things. That's the problem, for a while we do great and then it all goes down the drain.

Our intentions are first-rate but our actions are what ruins it. Once we see that the world judges us by our actions and not our intentions, the picture isn't very pretty. I always judged myself by my intentions, never by my actions. I realized I never had an accurate picture of myself. But once I started to look at myself in this reality, I saw the real picture. It wasn't a nice one.

Now we can let this go. We're going to place the whole package in the hands of our Higher Power. He's going to decide if we live sober or die drunk. We're going to stop fighting, that's all. No more bargains.

In my case, how many times did I promise God if he would get me out of this mess I would never do it again? I would straighten out my act. The odd thing was I would get out of the jackpot just to fall into another one. And I kept doing it time and time again.

So now we stop making deals.

This is the Golden Key to easy, contented sobriety. An active surrender to a Power greater than ourselves. This is how it really works. When my sponsor showed me how step three worked, I was set free. As odd as it may sound, my sobriety was no longer any of my business. It was His. I surrendered it into His hands.

My job from now on was to show up every day for the work He put in front of me. Whether my work was to get out of bed and do the dishes, clean the house, or just go to work, that was my job. My job now is to be honest and stop avoiding reality. To stand up as a human being and start moving ahead in this life. To be a father or whatever I am supposed to be. It's time for me to grow up.

Perhaps you're wondering if you're capable of being honest with yourself. You've heard the phrase "constitutionally capable of being honest with yourself" and wondered perhaps if you are capable of real self-honesty.

You are. Constitutionally capable just means you have enough mental capacity to know the difference between right and wrong.

You'll meet some people that have mental challenges in the program but they managed to get sober as long as they have the ability to know the difference between a lie and the truth.

Now, here's your time of decision. As it says in the book "we stood at the turning point". Remember half measures will avail us nothing, we are either in or out.

All you have to do is say it. Say it to the Higher Power you started with in Step Two.

At this point I'm going to recommend that you actually memorize the Third Step prayer from the big book. It is the most unselfish prayer I have ever come across since I got sober and it's very effective.

Read this with me out loud, and if it will help you, write it down so you can learn to memorize it. Write it out as many times as it takes.

"God, I offer myself to Thee. To build with me and to do with me as Thou wilt. Relieve me of the bondage of self, that I may better do Thy will. Take away my difficulties, that victory over them may bear witness to those I would help of Thy power, Thy love, and Thy way of life. May I do Thy will always!"

Do your very best to learn this prayer so you can say it every morning. It will help you more than I can tell you in the days ahead.

Then at night find something to be grateful for in your day. It doesn't matter what it is, it doesn't have to be something great, it could even be something small. But find *something* to express gratitude about. It is very important.

I'll warn you now, there will be days you're going to have difficulty finding something to be grateful for. That's not unusual, that's life. However, it is critical that you find something to verbally express gratitude about. Make it real.

I promise you if you do this every day for 90 days your life will change. You will come into fellowship with your Higher Power in a very real way. Just wait and see.

In this chapter on page 62 there are some examples of how to consider the God of your understanding.

Some are; He is the father; we are His children. Another is that He's our employer and He will provide what we need as long as we keep close to Him. That one is my favorite.

I now live in total expectancy of my needs being met. I need work, I need food, I need money to pay the bills.

I need to learn how to be the person I was meant to be and I need to be healthy. These are only a few of my needs, however they are not in my hands to supply. They are in His.

Since I have been on this path, He has never let me down, not once. Sometimes the answer didn't come in the way I expected or wanted but when it came it was effective and got the job done.

I'll admit it was pretty scary in the beginning, living by faith. But as time went by, I got better at it once I saw He was there for me.

Maybe right now this sounds scary to you however you need to keep in mind millions of people have been doing this. Not only in AA but even in religious organizations all over the world.

Even though we are not religious, we seek the same thing. To have a good life. To be of real help to people, and to be a better person than we are or have been.

This will require a five-letter word were not used to using, Truth. Telling the truth when it would be easier to lie. The only exception being "except when to do so would injure them or others." We don't lie but we also don't hurt people just so we can feel better.

You'll find it's uncomfortable sometimes to tell the truth but there's an important principle I have learned.

Do what's uncomfortable first and comfortable things will follow. If you only do what's comfortable now, uncomfortable things will follow.

If you apply that principle to all areas of your life, things will change drastically for you. It will not be easy but it will be rewarding.

So the only battle you will probably have for now, will be with your mind. Your mind may tell you that you don't have to do that, or this is a bunch of malarkey. Or maybe it will use a different word.

That will be the real battle. You must remember now that you are no longer alone. Speak out against those negative thoughts, openly deny them. If you hear a thought that says your worthless simply say out loud, "that's not true"!

Talk to your Higher Power, rely on the characteristics you gave him. Especially if they are power, love, and strength. He will not let you down, just stay close.

Remember that when it comes to the mind, you are in control. But in the beginning of sobriety your mind will be like a wild horse. It will be bucking and kicking at every step you take. Just take control, you are the boss and keep your Higher Power with you at all times.

When I first started my mind was out to get me. I thought I was going insane. I couldn't drink anymore to make the voices go away, and now they were going wild.

As a direct result of doing these 12 steps these voices have disappeared. They no longer run my life, keep me up at night, or interfering with me from hearing people talk because their voices were so loud.

I think this was the first big miracle that happened in my recovery. That my head finally shut off! What a miracle that was, what a joy. Now I have a chance. I'm not fighting against myself anymore, I'm working with myself in a positive way that works!

Once you've said the third step prayer, you're done!

Step three is complete.

Congratulations!

However, in order for this step to take hold in your sobriety you must launch into your personal house cleaning which is Step 4. No hesitation.

You said you were willing to go to any length to get sober right? Then grab a piece of paper right now and just write out the first resentment that comes to mind. I'm sure that will be no problem. Something will come to mind immediately, just write it down. It doesn't have to be a book, just start with the first one that comes to mind. If you feel like writing a few more, go for it.

Step Four

Congratulations on making it to Step Four!

I want you to know that I'm proud of you and you're not alone doing this. Your Higher Power will be with you all the way through it.

Let's get started.

"Made a searching and fearless moral inventory of ourselves".

Step four is our demonstration to our Higher Power that we're willing to do what it takes to get sober. The purpose of step four is to get rid of the things inside that are blocking the sunlight of The Spirit.

So this is our course. As it said in Step Three:

*"**Next** we launched out on a course of vigorous action, the first step of which is a personal housecleaning, which many of us had never attempted. Though our decision was a vital and crucial step, it could have a little permanent effect unless at once followed by a strenuous effort to face, and be rid of, the things in ourselves which had been blocking us."*

Did you notice the promise that was inside that last paragraph? Doing your fourth step will have a ***permanent effect*** on you and the rest of your sobriety? Many people don't see that promise, but it's yours to have. And it rocks! It's a life changer.

I'll be honest with you, I had a little bit of fear doing a step four. I had been hiding from things that happened to me in my past for many years. I held shame, anger, and fear as my armor any time someone got close to me. It ruined a lot of relationships.

No more!

One of the very important aspects of this book points out that we do a *yearly* inventory. Just like a business has to do a yearly inventory, we do the same with ourselves. In fact, it says a business must do a yearly inventory just to survive as a business. Our Big Book says "**we did <u>exactly</u> the same thing with our lives**". When taking inventory, we need to evaluate what is called the stock in trade. This can relate to the character defects and even abilities we use to shield ourselves from the world. It reads: "he cannot fool himself about values."

Don't become concerned if you find that statement a little bit overwhelming. Remember the book says that "***the point is** we are **willing to grow** along spiritual lines, the principles we have set down our guides to progress. We claim spiritual progress rather than spiritual perfection.*" So, we are not going to get drunk if we don't do an inventory every year, but we must be **willing** to grow. That's all. I find that I need to do the 12 steps again once every 2 to 4 years. Once I start losing my patience again, I know it's time for another inventory. But I go through the entire 12 steps again as it is a process. Each step builds on the other.

Remember, as it says, we're not Saints. Plus, this process of discovery will get far easier once you see and experience the rewards. There will be plenty of them.

As we move forward in our sobriety, we will discover more and more about ourselves deep within. Just like the layers of an onion, these layers will fall away until we get to the core within. With an onion you'll notice the first layer comes off easy. It's all dried out and you can easily see the dark color of it. Then as you take off more layers you sense a slimy feeling to the beginning layers underneath. Then the deeper you go the color gets clearer and cleaner. The core will be a clean clear color, but it takes time to get there.

Perhaps as you are exposing the layers within yourself, your eyes may tear up the same way you would with an onion when you peel it. It's perfectly normal if it happens.

It is important I tell you something about your inventory at this point.

It **must be** a complete account of everything. Nothing left out. If you do leave things out *it won't work for you*. You may be tempted in the area where we discuss our sexual issues to leave things out. Don't do it. Half measures availed us nothing, remember? So let's dump this garbage and move on with life the way it should be. Free of the past and ready for tomorrow!

This is the only time we're going to go back through our lives. To the earliest memory we have of any situation we can remember. We will never have to go back through our full life ever again. The only exception to that would be if we remembered something later and needed to discuss it. Otherwise it's a one-time trip to this time in our life. Then the next time we do our steps, in a few years, we start from where we left off.

Yes, we're going to be writing a lot, but that's okay. We're cleaning house, right? We are going to get started in the basement where it's dark and damp and clean it all out so it's presentable. We will expose it to the light of Truth.

Besides, the basement holds the foundation to the whole house. We are going to open the windows and let the light in. Let in the fresh air and kick out all the creepy crawlies. They don't belong in our house anymore!

As a direct result of doing this you will be given another promise from the Big Book. You will be "*rocketed to a dimension of living of which we had never dreamed.*"

Wait till that one happens!

Like it says in this chapter, this is a fact facing process. We are not looking to place guilt or blame, we are looking at aspects of your ego though self. Once you've done that, just consider how it's evident in your life today, that's it.

That was easy.

Now, (if you're using the online Big Book) go to the page labeled 8 of 14 in the chapter of How it Works. Or page 65 in the Big Book.

You'll see it will be laid out in the perfect way to list resentments.

I'm resentful at, then **the Cause**, and then, **Affects my**:

The only thing I'm going to ask you to do is add a number for each one.

So Mr. Brown would be #1

Mrs. Jones is #2 and so on.

This will help you later on in the step. If you remember something about a resentment you had already listed (for example Mrs. Jones) just list it with the same number but add an "a" or "b" as needed. Example: Mrs. Jones #2a. She lied about knowing me.

It's important to understand that resentments are not only about anger. They can be about embarrassment, regret, and even fear.

You can have resentments against people you love as well as resentments against yourself. This does not take away from the love you have for these people however you need to get these resentments out.

I had resentments against God. That he would allow things to happen to me when I was a child. It was important that I exposed those feelings as well. Besides you can't have a good relationship with someone if you're not honest with them, right?

So we start from the beginning, our earliest memory that comes to mind. Perhaps you were punished for something you did. Whether you deserved it or not you can add it to your list if it's been something you have thought about it since it happened in your childhood.

The translation of the word resentment is, to re-think or re-feel a prior situation. So if you find a memory keeps coming up every once in a while we write it down.

If you're not sure, write it down anyway, just to be thorough.

So you write down the first part, *I'm resentful at*. Then under I'm resentful at, the person. Maybe your dad, your mom, or guardian, or even the school principal. I got strap from lots of vice principals who were nuns when I was a kid.

Then next to the cause you write how it affected you. This part you're going to need to keep brief. All you need is a short note that will remind you of the incident. Perhaps, as an example, when I did mine I wrote, they strapped me so hard my hands were numb. Or she made me cry and I was embarrassed. Just try to keep it brief, you can relate the whole story later.

Then beside that, "affects my", we will write what it affects. This is the list of affects we will use.

Self-esteem [how I feel about myself]

Ambitions [things I wanted to have or do later were affected]

Security [did I feel insecure after this?]

Personal relationship [was my friendship affected with anyone?]

Sex relations [was I affected sexually in any way, sex relationships]

So we do this with each one. Number it, what the cause is, and how it affects me.

Sometimes with the "affects" area we may have some trouble. But do your best. Ask yourself, did this affect how I felt about myself? (self-esteem) or were my personal relationships with them or other people affected? If it was, just add it to the list.

Doing this portion of step four can sometimes take a few days to a week or more. Especially your first step four. So do what you can right now by writing down what comes to mind. You can go on as long as you wish. But I want you to do a little bit every single day.

IMPORTANT

You will need to keep a small notepad with you along with a pen or pencil during the day. The reason why is you're going to start remembering things you had forgotten about even if it was many years ago. If you don't write these down you'll forget them again. So don't go anywhere without your little pad and writing utensil.

As it says in the book, *"nothing counts more than thoroughness and honesty, we go back through our lives holding nothing back."*

We will be covering People, places and things in our inventory. When it comes to "things" you can even have fun with this part.

Believe it or not, my toaster was on my first inventory. The bloody thing wouldn't pop the toast up. I had to babysit it. Guess what? It almost always burnt my toast (which I hated) and I wound up throwing the burnt toast out and going without breakfast. Great way to start the day, hungry and angry.

Funny thing was, I discovered something very interesting as a result of putting "things" in my inventory.

Once you've written down all you can and you can't think of anything else we will move onto the next section. Just leave some empty space at the end in case you remember something later. Then just add it to the list.

Once you have written everything you can think of, turn to page 66 of the Big Book and 3/4's of the way down the page you'll find an important promise.

"We turned back to the list, for it held the keys to the future."

This particular part will be responsible for giving you a new future. So stay on the path.

First, we see that people who wronged us were perhaps spiritually sick. So right here we turn to our Higher Power and ask for the strength to show these people the same tolerance, pity, and patience we would *cheerfully* grant a sick friend.

This is not something we can do of our own will. It must come from Him because we are under the influence of the resentment and the limited power of self. So we ask for our Higher Power's strength to do this. So if you want to say a small prayer asking for this ability right now. I'll wait...

Once you have done this we can look at what to do next.

Remember that I asked you to number the resentments? This is why.

Now we are going to write out *OUR* part in the situation. This is **not about** looking to blame or guilting yourself into something, it is only a way to see what our role MAY HAVE been.

In some resentments of the past you may not have had any part in it at all.

When I was a child I was abused by my step-father. I had no fault in that, but as I grew up I began to steal from him. Then I carried hate towards him for a lot of years. That was MY part *afterwards*.

But by living in the anger the abuse caused I was allowing the abuse to continue into my adult years! He was dead and I'm still living in a furious resentment. It had to stop. It had to be released from ruining my life years after it happened. It was screwing up my relationships with people I cared about and the ones I fell in love with.

Just so you know, as a result of doing this, this continuing resentment was removed.

Ok, so let's look at the resentment you numbered as #1.

You'll start a new list and for each resentment you're going to ask these questions.

Where was I selfish, dishonest, self-seeking (looking for pity for ourselves or anger towards the offenders from others) and frightened?

So you could write something like:

(If the resentment was the abuse of my step-father)

I was selfish because now that I am in a new relationship I don't care about the feelings of my partner. I am only concerned that my rules are met or else.

I am self-seeking because I told people about this abuse so they would be angry at him along with me which strengthened my cause and justified my resenting him.

I am frightened because this injury isn't going away. I lived with the memory for years. I suspected others of abuse just because I felt like it. Then I could re-justify my feelings. The pain just went around and around.

It's critical you DO NOT mention the person you are resentful at in any way in this part of the inventory. This *has to be* your side of the street (so to speak) only. His or her part of this is not mentioned in any way. So work hard to make sure they are not mentioned in this part of it.

Just look at your side and keep them out of it entirely. You will be tempted to put them in this part of the inventory to justify your feelings, but you must focus only on you. It's very important!

This part of the inventory literally gives you a new future. It did for me in a huge way.

Here's one:

I used to feel guilty for things I *didn't* do. If someone came into the room and said someone broke into their car during the night, I would feel guilty. But I didn't do it!

Then some moron would say "You wouldn't feel guilty if you didn't do it". So you now add confusion to the guilt.

What a mess.

This went on for years. However, it was removed from me as a direct result of this process, so stick with me and just be thorough, ok?

You'll be writing a lot, but it's worth it. Make sure you do something every day. Write at least one resentment down each day. More is better, but at least one! Remember we stay sober one day at a time, so let's do our part each day with this until we're ready to move on to the next phase.

At this point I want to give you a little encouragement.

Just in Step 4, there are 24 promises that will come true for you as a result of you doing this inventory. Twenty-four! You'll be able to see them later as you get better reading the book and seeing the promises it relates to you.

So stay on the path and let nothing stop you, nothing!

So once you are ready, we will do a simple part of Step 4.

It says on page 67 "*notice the word Fear*" is in the AFFECTS MY section? It shows us that fear has become a major part of our lives. Anger is an outcome of fear among other things. We get angry at little things. Blow up or yell at people who may care about us. Then we feel regret for it.

So looking at the list where the anger part comes up, write down a fear list.

Mine was something like.

I'm afraid of my anger. I'm afraid of loving someone, trusting anyone. I'm afraid of being honest, (people will find out what happened to me) doing a 4th step because it might not work for me, and on and on.

It won't take long but it will help you to see how fear is in control of your life.

Now to get rid of the fear. Yes, have it removed!

Maybe not right away, but some will disappear right away. It's up to your Higher Power. We are going to give this anger to Him. We will say in our way, a small prayer to ask Him to give us the tolerance and patience needed to deal with this fear.

The cool thing is we will let God demonstrate through us what He can do.

Here's a promise that will be yours once you finish this talk (prayer) with Him. It's near the bottom of page 68.

"**At once, we commence to outgrow fear**." (!!!!) This has come true for those that simply allow it to happen. As it says, we are now on different footing.

Ok, ready for the next part? We're getting close to the finish line. You are doing great. Your Higher Power is with you. You are not alone in this.

The next part is about sex.

We keep this part simple and don't try to justify or explain anything. We just write it out. It's important to know that sex problems are a normal problem that a lot of people have. The Big Book even goes as far to say we would hardly be human if we didn't have sex problems.

That's one thing I had never been called, human! Or at least I didn't feel human. So that sentence helped me quite a bit. Like I said, my mind loved to torment me and sex was a great topic for it.

So what we do here is simply look at our own sex conduct over the past and apply these questions to each situation.

Where had **we** been selfish, dishonest, or inconsiderate?

Whom had **we** hurt?

Did **we** unjustifiably arouse jealousy, suspicion or bitterness?

Where were **we** at fault, what could we have done instead?

So with each situation we apply those questions. Then once we're done, we take a look at it. This helps us to shape a better ideal for us to try to live up to. At this point we talk to our Higher Power again.

"We asked God to mold our ideas and help us to live up to them. We remembered always that are sex powers were God given and therefore good, neither to be used lightly or selfishly nor to be despised and loathed."

It's important that in your heart you must have a desire to want to live up to these ideals. When you are confronted with a situation where sex may become involved simply ask God to give you some direction. The right answer will come if you want to live up to your ideal. That's it.

Guess what?

You're done! You did it!

Good job. You've left nothing out.

If you want to have a little talk with your Higher Power and give thanks for getting this far. Go for it. Many of us tried to do a Step 4 but gave up when the going got tough. You didn't. I am proud of you, really!

What you have done here is shown your Higher Power you're willing to do what it takes. You've taken action!

This concludes your Step Four.

Congratulations. You've made it to;

Step Five

"**Admitted to God, to ourselves, and to another human being the exact nature of our wrongs.**"

There are some wonderful promises in this step when we do our part.

One of them (in relation to our character defects) is: "***Now these are about to be cast out.***"

I'll let you in on one of my most troublesome defects when I first started the program. I was a thief. It was an addiction that I couldn't control. I stole from friends, family, stores, you name it. If it wasn't tied down it was in my pocket.

This led to a lot of guilt. Especially when I stole from friends. Here I am sober (mostly because I wanted to stay out of jail) and I have an uncontrollable defect of stealing. There was no forethought as to the consequences of getting caught at all. Just a driving urge to steal.

After I had done my first 4th step I found that I had received a conscience! It was amazing. Something wonderful happened inside of me that gave me forethought before I would act on taking anything. Yes, the thought to take things would still happen but now I have another thought or voice that speaks out before I do anything!

I can't express in words how grateful I was to God for His intercession with this defect. Not even close. It felt like I had been saved from impending doom. It was only a matter of time till I would get caught again. I knew the odds.

Occasionally a thought will enter my mind to grab some stupid item I'm not even interested in, but now other thought comes to mind and it would talk it over with me. It could be a simple thought that just says the item does not belong to me. Like, this would be stealing, or I would have to make amends if I did take something that wasn't mine.

The miracle is, I NEVER had these types of thoughts before, never! They are a welcome barrier to the addiction of stealing that was one of my worst defects growing up.

I wanted to share that with you because you may have a particular defect or *shortcoming* (I'll cover what a shortcoming is in step 7) that will just be removed immediately, while others will be removed later.

The only reason I could find for some defects not being removed right way is that in some cases I needed to learn something important. In other defects, people needed to see that His power is real. Remember the 3rd Step prayer? **"Take away my difficulties that victory over them may bear witness to those that I would help of Thy Love and Power..."**

It was this particular defect that made me finally do the 12 steps.

I would go to the meeting and say everything was great, and then go home to the incessant ranting of my thoughts. Unable to sleep and unable to shut them off. It was horrible. I really thought I was going to go nuts or just end it all. It was that bad.

As I said, it was this particular defect a character of stealing that caused me to seek out a sponsor and finally do the 12 steps.

I was four years without a drink and going to meetings pretty regularly. I knew how to talk the "AA way" so I would fit in, but it was just talk. I hadn't done the steps, or approached anyone to see if they would sponsor me. I was more interested in getting a girl.

One particular day I needed some groceries so I went to the local supermarket. I remember going to the meat department and seeing a really nice T-bone steak but it was too expensive for me so I couldn't get it.

Later when I was in the aisle for toiletries, I grabbed a pack of razor blades for my shaver. When I saw the price for them, I was appalled. They were almost five dollars just for a pack of razor blades!

Then the committee of idiots in my head came to order. They said to me that I could sneak those razor blades into my pocket and no one would see me. I was good at it, I had shoplifted for years and I knew I wouldn't get caught. Then I could go down to that meat deli get myself that T-bone steak. The committee of idiots in my head said I deserved it!

So I listened to them. I slipped that package of razor blades into my jacket with real finesse and trotted off to the meat deli to get that T-bone steak. I think I even felt good about it!

Perhaps I should mention at this point that I had a record of criminal activity that went back 10 years. Getting caught doing anything illegal, especially with my record, would mean immediate and substantial jail time.

But did this occur to me? Nope, not for one second.

I went to the cashier and paid for everything that was in my shopping cart and walked out to my car.

Then once I got into my car, my sanity returned. I was in a panic. What the hell did I just do? How could I have done something so stupid? I wasn't even thinking of the consequences! I was really, really scared. I stopped drinking and joined AA so I wouldn't have to worry about getting drunk and into trouble again. Now I'm sober (or dry) for 4 years and I'm stealing with no thought of the consequences? Like I said, at this moment I was terrified. I had no defense against my behaviors either. My life was unmanageable, sober!

It was at that time that I told God what to do. It was the first (and last) time I ever did this.

This is what I said: "God I'm going to go to an AA meeting and find someone who can take me through the 12 steps. I want someone there who knows how to do them. I will do them to the best of my ability and if it doesn't work, I'm out! It's the only thing I haven't tried." Or something very close to it.

In this city the AA program was twelve-step oriented. Every meeting you went to they talked about the 12 Steps, it was almost nauseating at the time. Thank God for that.

I went to a meeting that evening to look for someone that could take me through the 12 steps.

During that meeting a native man was sitting in the corner and he was talking about sex problems. It was hilarious to listen to him. Everybody was laughing their heads off but he was speaking sincere truth. He was talking about the thoughts and feelings he had during his day. It was so funny to hear that kind of insanity.

What was different about this though, I had the exact same thoughts and feelings. Except I was scared to death that anyone else would know about them!

I wanted what he had. Freedom from self. I was living inside a prison in my mind and from my thoughts.

They were in control of me and I wasn't even drinking anymore!

I approached him after the meeting, told him what happened, and said I needed a sponsor. The short part of the story was he agreed to help me through the steps and my life changed from that point on.

I really didn't plan to get into that story as part of Step Five however I wanted to relate how unmanageable my life was. At this point I really didn't understand how powerless I was over alcohol, but I thought I was going insane because of this mental unmanageability in my life.

I want you to know, as I mentioned earlier, some defects may be removed immediately, while others will be removed over time. But I promise you it will happen.

Okay, back on track.

First, **under no circumstance** do you destroy your fourth step list once you're done. You will need it for steps six, seven, and eight. So **do not destroy it!**

The reason I mention this is because many times the priest or the person you do the fifth step with it tells you can destroy your 4th step list. Do not do it, you will need it to make your list!

As I mentioned earlier, I suggested you speak to some people in your group and ask them if they know of a priest that does 5th steps. If someone recommends a person, great. Give them a call and set up an appointment. Don't dawdle on this, make the call and set up an appointment you can go to. Make sure your afternoon (or morning) is free, because it may take a while to get it done.

Your goal when you go to talk to this person is to reveal the nature of your behaviors during the past. If you discovered you've been a liar, a thief, a person that preys on others, whatever, you're going to talk about it.

You'll discuss what you found out about yourself. Perhaps that some of these situations were actually your fault. That perhaps you set the ball in motion. Or perhaps now you have behaviors as a result of what happened to you in the past.

Whatever it is, discuss it all.

Under no circumstance do you hold anything back. You will be tempted to keep quiet about something you've been keeping a secret for most of your life. Don't do it. If you do this, all your work, it will all be for nothing. The process will not work.

I had situations that happen to me when I was young and when I was a young teenager. I was very embarrassed and angry about and I didn't want to discuss it.

Thankfully my sponsor pointed out earlier that if I held anything back there was no point in doing this Fifth Step at all. Realize the importance of going for it 100%.

Once you have completed your Fifth Step go home and take a look at the prior four steps you have done just to make sure you've done your best with them. Then have a talk with your Higher Power and give thanks for getting this far.

If you're lucky enough to be able to get to a meeting, do it. Just sit and listen and enjoy being in the company of people who want to stay sober. If you're asked to contribute or share, keep it simple and do it with gratitude.

Don't look for lightning out of the sky or the clouds parting with Angels singing. It's not going to happen. But as I promised earlier what you have done today is going to have a permanent effect on the rest of your life. You'll see changes as time goes by, some will be pretty amazing, I promise!

Ok, if you're done, good work. Keep talking to the God your understanding. Keep Him close. You're in the trenches now and battling against your enemy. God will be there to help, even if you have your own panel of idiots in your head.

You are no longer alone.

Have a good night's sleep my friend, you deserve it.

We can start on 6 & 7 tomorrow...

Step Six

"Were entirely ready to have God remove all these defects of character."

I'm sure you will hear some people say there's no difference between steps 6 and 7. Or even that they made a mistake giving them different numbers. I have even heard people say they are both about the same thing. Nothing could be further from the truth.

Actually, they are complete opposites!

This was mentioned by Bill Wilson in a discussion he had with long time member Chuck C. before they both passed on.

Now let's look at Step 6.

The step(s) are covered on page 76 in your Big Book of Alcoholics Anonymous.

The emphasis is again stated that willingness is the key so we can now **let** God remove all things (we found in our 4th step) we found objectionable.

As you may have discovered, some of the items you discovered in your inventory are items you use to defend yourself. To be used as some sort of armor. Anger is a great one. We can turn from a quiet unassuming person to a person in rage as soon as someone gets close to us. We don't want to be hurt or discovered as vulnerable so we have a wall of anger to protect us.

This is just an example.

With me, anger was a switch inside of me that I lived in fear of. If someone took me to a specific point in my anger the switch would get thrown and I was in an uncontrollable rage.

Once I jumped out of a truck going 40 miles an hour to avoid lashing out at the fellow who was blaming me for behaviors he was actually responsible for!

I had seconds to react because I was at the explosion point. This had been going on for weeks and now he was saying he was tired of doing my work! He sat in his truck all day and did nothing, and yet he was now saying he was fed up with my lack of responsibility.

It was either severely damage this guy, or jump out of the truck. I chose the latter.

Of course he pulled over to see if I was ok but all I could do was yell at him to get away from me before I did something I regretted.

I had to take a couple days off work and get to some meetings to settle down. But that's how bad it was. I had not done my steps yet at this point in my sobriety. I was like a wandering grenade waiting to explode.

However, after I had completed the 12 Steps a few times over the years this anger is no longer so volatile. For all intents and purposes this "switch" has disappeared. Thank God!

So Step 6 is for our character defects. The things **we do**.

We lie, cheat, steal or become dishonest, if that is what you discovered in your 4th Step list. Perhaps you discovered some self-defense mechanisms you use when people "get too close" or begin to challenge you at times.

Now we approach the God of our present understanding and voice the words that we are now ready for Him to remove these character defects. Even the ones we use to protect ourselves. No reservation, we are now entirely ready to be vulnerable and count on His protection when needed.

In the next chapter there is also a prayer you can use if you need help voicing your desire for release.

That will complete your step 6!

Step Seven

Step 7 is about our shortcomings. This is where we *come up short* on the needed power to do what we should be doing. The things **we don't do.**

Let's say you are consistently late for work, or you're slow to clean your home or apartment. You come up short on the desire or willingness to do the things you need to do as an adult. I'm sure you can find some of these types of shortcomings in your own life. One for me was I always came up short on patience. I would shoot my mouth off in the worst of times.

With these issues we need His help to inspire or motivate us to do the things we should be doing as a responsible sober person. You could even add going to more meetings to that list. If that is an issue of course.

You can say this prayer from our book when you are willing to let go of these defects and shortcomings:

"My creator, I am now willing that you should have all of me, good and bad. I pray that you now remove from me every single defect of character which stands in the way of my usefulness to you and my fellows. Grant me strength, as I go out from here, to do your bidding. Amen"

This is the two sides of the same coin.

The things we do, and the things we don't do, that need to be done. That's about as complete as anything can be. Nothing is left out.

Although covering these two steps is brief, don't underestimate their importance. They make up the prescription to a sober future and a vibrant relationship with your Higher Power.

When you're ready you can move on to Step 8. A day or two is fine.

Step Eight

"Made a list of all persons we had harmed, and became willing to make amends to the all."

Again, I congratulate you on your progress and willingness to go to any length to get sober.

Actually, that is a spiritual principle that is thousands of years old. The principal is that if you are will to go to any length you can have anything thing you want. If you have a burning desire to achieve something, and have God on your side, nothing can stop you.

I'll let you in on a secret.

You can be willing to go to any length, but you don't actually **have to** go to any length. As long as *the willingness* is there in your heart and mind, the goal is open to achieve.

Step 8 is structured around this 2,000-year-old spiritual principal.

On page 76 in your Big Book it briefly covers Step 8 and 9. However we need to scrutinize the last word in Step Eight.

"Made a list of all persons we had harmed and became willing to make amends to them all".

That word "all" is the clincher. This is the one that separates the men from the boys. The women from the girls. You must be WILLING to make amends to *every single person* in your list, no exceptions!

Let me give an example;

In my case I had committed a crime while I was drunk and I was found "not guilty" of the charge when I went to court.

For me to be able to move on to Step nine I had to be WILLING to go to the police and inform them I was the person guilty of that crime. No con job to make it easier, just fess up and tell them it was me.

I realized that if I didn't get sober, I was doomed to repeat my actions, drunk or sober anyways! At least if I stayed sober, I had a chance at life.

Pay attention to what I am about to say **please**. You do not HAVE TO do this, (go to the police) but you must be WILLING TO. That's the key!

Because of this, I needed a couple days to search my heart and mind for this willingness to go to *any length* to stay sober. Finally, after I thought long and hard over it, I knew the only recourse for me was to be willing to go to any length by getting honest no matter the cost.

Then, once I could honestly say I was willing to go to this length, THEN I could move on to Step nine. Not until then.

Here's a saying that relates to this process you will go through with Step 8.

"The difference between iron and steel is fire. Fire tempers the iron into steel and makes it more valuable and much stronger."

Feel the heat?

Go for it, search and find the willingness. The outcome will be strength and self-worth.

This is a big one. Once you see the value, you will understand the cost of doing this step the way it is intended.

Now spend some time meditating on this step and search your heart. Search your mind and think it through. The Truth is waiting for you.

Step Nine

"Made direct amends to such people wherever possible, except when to do so would injure them or others."

Good work!

You found the willingness to go to any length to get sober and made it through the crunch of Step eight as it was revealed to you in the prior chapter. Awesome.

Now we are ready to have the rubber hit the road. To walk the talk, to get action into our Steps.

I want to tell you something very important at this point. When you are going out to make amends, your Higher Power will be there with you. He will be there in powerful ways because you are walking into unknown territory now. Possibly you have never done anything like this before. Perhaps you're a little hesitant or maybe even scared.

Just put those fears aside and do it anyway. That's what fearlessness is. To do something in spite of the fear. It does not mean you have no fear. It means that you do it anyways.

When I was doing my first 9th Step I had one particular person that I was scared of making amends to. I had broken into his home and stolen some senseless items when I was drunk. He had just got married too.

This guy was a big fellow with attitude to match.

What I was afraid of was that he would punch me in the face the moment I approached him to make amends.

I deserved it. That's not what I was afraid of. I was afraid that I would not be able to take the punch and would get into a fight with him. I knew if I hit him my amends would go right out the window.

I prayed my butt off asking God to show me some kind of sign so I could skip doing amends with this guy. I just didn't want to screw it up. Well, you guessed it, He didn't send any signs to let me off the hook.

Funny thing happened though.

One day I'm walking through a shopping mall and as I walked around the corner, right in front of me was this guy! I froze.

Then I noticed that he had a little girl in one hand and a little boy with the other. All of a sudden, I heard a voice in my head that was unfamiliar to me.

"His hands are busy, do it now!"

I just walked right up to him and said: "Hi, I'm not sure if you remember me or not".

He looked me deep in the eyes and said: "Yeah, I remember you."

I said (before he could say anything else) "I want to apologize for what I did to you and you wife. I broke into your home and took your belongings. I am very sorry for doing that".

Then I did something important that my sponsor taught me.

Always try to leave the person feeling better than the way you found them.

I said: "At the same time I want to thank you. Because of you, my life has turned around. I'm sober 5 years now and I have a chance at leading a normal life. I wish it didn't happen the way it did, but I wanted to say that because of you, being in my life at that moment, that was the turning point for me. Maybe that isn't the most flattering thing to say to someone but I am truly grateful and I wanted to thank you for that. If I can pay for the damages I caused I would be happy to send you the money as soon as I can."

He looked at me kind of weird and held out his hand. I gratefully took his hand and shook it.

I thanked him for his time and wished him the best with his wife and family.

When I got into my car I was shaking with excitement and real gratitude. God had presented the situation so I could do the amends! **I had no doubt about it.** It was amazing. I was yelling "whoo hoo!" and banging around in the car like a little kid who just got his first bike. I'll never forget it.

I wanted to share that with you to give you an example that may help when you go out to make your own amends. I'm sure you'll hear about other miracles from speakers at some of your own meetings. Just have faith and get this done. Make sure your sponsor knows what you're doing at all times, if you have one.

Sometimes you may have difficulty making amends because the person may live far away. As long as you are willing to make the amends when the opportunity happens, you can put it off for now. You must be willing to do it however, as soon as the situation or person presents themselves.

If the person has passed on, you can go to the grave site and make the amends. Maybe even volunteer at a senior's home for a couple weeks or months as an effort to show your desire to make amends if the person was a senior. They don't have to know why you're volunteering.

If you were abusive to animals you can start a drive to raise money for homeless dogs or help people to get dog tags who can't afford them.

Get creative. The desire to make amends will inspire you to find a way, trust me. Just try to relate the amends to the situation from your 4th step.

One final point, **it's critical.**

You are not going out to make amends to get forgiveness. If they tell you to get lost or something worse it does not matter! Making the amends is what you are there for. You are there to make genuine amends.

If the person accepts your amends, great. But if they do not, **it does not matter!** Thank them for their time and move on. If you're angry over what they said back to you, talk to your Higher Power for strength to forgive them. Maybe they've been angry a long time and can't get over it right away just because you apologized. You certainly can't blame them for their feelings. They could have been holding the injury of your actions for a long time.

Remember, we must be hard on ourselves but always tolerant of others. We must. Prayer will help in these situations so apply when needed!

Remember what I told you about leaving a person feeling better that the way you found them?

My sponsor always left a person feeling better than the way he found them. That is easy when they are already happy, but your work is cut out for you if they are angry.

As long as you are genuine it has a good chance of working out. Do you best and say a little prayer for them if you were unsuccessful afterwards. They'll need it. So will you.

Alright, get to work and stay on track. Good things will happen. This 9th step may have some bumps when you do it but you will not be alone on this ride. And you will never be alone again either. Just as a side note, step nine is where you get your "conscious contact" promise that is mentioned in Step 11!

Step 10

"Continued to take personal inventory and when we were wrong promptly admitted it."

I had an unusual situation happen to me with Step ten.

I was involved in a men's Big Book Study where we not only studied but "lived" the steps we were on for that week of the study. My sponsor ran the group and he suggested that each week we keep our eyes and ears open to see how the week went in relation to the step we were on at the time. That's what I meant by *lived* that step for the week.

Oddly enough, each week we were on a step, something significant happened in direct relation to the particular step I was on at the time.

All the way from Step 1 to Step 9, someone said something or something happened that week that directly related to the step I was on for that week. It was almost eerie.

All except for step 10.

Absolutely nothing happened that was related to Step 10 that week. It was like everything went quiet. I didn't do anything different either. Went to the same meetings, went to work, everything. Then once we moved on to Step 11 occurrences started up again in direct relation to Step 11. This went on until we had completed the study.

What I interpreted that to mean was that the 10th step was my job. Something I was responsible for. I needed to be able to end my day with the approval of my conscience before I hit the pillow. I needed to evaluate my day with a short inventory of questions.

It says;

"Continue to watch for selfishness, dishonesty, resentment, and fear. When these crop up, we ask God at once to remove them."

Step 10 begins on page 84 to the bottom of 85 of the Big Book. In these two pages you will find 6 different promises of what has or will happen because of the course you are on.

Some of these are:

"We have entered the world of the spirit.

For by this time sanity (balance) will have returned. (You're not even done yet!)

We will see that our new attitude toward liquor has been given us without any thought or effort on our part.

We are not fighting it, neither are we avoiding temptation. Instead the problem has been removed. It does not exist for us.

We are not cured of alcoholism. What we really have is a daily reprieve contingent on the maintenance of our spiritual condition. (Look up the definition of reprieve!)

If we have carefully followed directions, we have begun to sense the flow of His Spirit into us.

To some extent we have become God-conscious."

These are powerful statements. The one that hit me hardest was that God was now a part of my **conscious** mind. I tried to have God in mind before, but I just couldn't maintain that desire. The insanity of my mind would push out any thoughts like that.

Now it comes automatically.

There was a movie I watched once called "Fearless "and Jeff Bridges was the main actor. He had an intense fear of flying.

For some reason he had to take this flight and he couldn't get out of it. During the flight, the plane began to fall out of the sky. The plane was even coming apart as it was falling. Seats were being sucked out of the side of the aircraft where the side had broken away. He would turn and see people flying out the airplane as the plane was falling.

    The scene was total chaos. I think he actually changed his seat with a friend earlier in his row and that person was sucked out of the airplane. As the plane was falling you could see in his face that he was losing it. But all of a sudden everything in the scene went into slow motion.

    More people were flying out of the airplane, and people being killed by debris, and the insanity of the whole situation was easy to see.

    But all of a sudden, he entered into a state of euphoria, or even peace. For him, all of a sudden, everything was okay. It looks like he had accepted he was going to die and he was okay with it.

    Shortly afterwards the scene cuts to where you see him walking in the cornfield. He was in a daze. The plane had crashed but somehow, he had survived. The unusual thing was he was still in a state of peace.

    Later on, in the movie his insurance agent wanted him to add extra drama to the story of his friend dying and his near-death experience for the courts. All with the intent of getting more money from the insurance companies.

But he got really upset because he didn't want to lie. Somehow, he knew that dishonesty would end his peaceful euphoric state.

He ran to the top of the building and stood up on the edge of the roof, inches from death. It's this scene that is shown on the cover for the movie. He has his hands outstretched and his head back with the wind blowing through his hair. He thought he could get his serenity back if he went to the edge of dying again.

I don't want to give too much of it away but it's an excellent movie. I highly recommend you take the time to see it. I found it to be a profoundly spiritual movie, but that was my perspective.

Oddly enough the same things can and will happen to you once you follow these directions for a while. As you progress along this path, especially doing a step ten each day, you won't be able to allow dishonesty into your sobriety. It just won't fit.

You will find yourself upset and distracted by allowing old behaviors into your new way of living. They just don't mix.

This is a huge benefit as a result of doing a Step ten when you retire for the day.

Take a few minutes to review your day. Again, were there any situations where you were selfish, dishonest, resentful, or fearful? It may be a little difficult, and you may even be tired. But don't let your head tell you you'll do it later, do it now. BEFORE you put your head to the pillow. It will only take a couple minutes and you need to do it each night.

What's cool about this is it will become almost automatic. You won't have to search your day to find out where you been dishonest or selfish or self-seeking, it won't matter. Because if you allow any old behaviors to come into your new life, you just won't feel right. Even if you don't know what it is, your internal system will be off center.

This is a good thing. Don't worry about turning into some kind of Saint. Just check when you're in the shower in the morning to see if you're standing on the water, or in it. If you're standing *in* the water, you're still human.

Just keep doing your step ten.

Remember now that God is your new fixer. Not alcohol. Alcohol removed your dignity, perhaps your job or family and more.

Now you have a better solution. One that will remove fear and resentments. He will bring you from darkness into light. He will make you better from the inside out. That's a promise.

That covers step 10.

Step Eleven

"Sought through prayer and meditation to improve our conscious contact with God as we understood Him, praying only for the knowledge of His will for us and the power to carry that out."

Wow, Step 11 already. How do you feel? Have you had some exciting things happen during your Steps so far? Did you have some bumps as you walked the path? Not to worry, I promised you are not alone and I would not say that if I didn't know it to be true. Honest.

Each of us has our own path. Our old ways will not always let us go that easily. Perhaps you have friends that you truly care about that you don't want to let go of.

What worked for me was to realize that if they were really my friends, they would understand and approve of what I was doing. They would give me the time to do this process and get better. Then later, once I have some spiritual strength, I can visit them again if I wanted to. Not so I could hang around and watch them drink. If that's their lifestyle it won't be a healthy environment for you. It's a prescription for eventual failure.

But if you like their friendship, get your head on straight and THEN renew the relationship. Once you've got your sober legs, you'll have some sanity, and if a scenario comes up that is unsafe for you, you'll know what to do.

There's no harm to say: Hey guys, gotta go. Have a good time.

If this relationship is a much closer one, like a girlfriend or even a spouse, that is different.

I will not suggest that you should leave your husband or wife if they are drinking and you are not. That is a decision you should discuss with not only with your sponsor but also a number of sober couples who know about this. And only if this is causing a lot of trouble for you. No one can make a judgment for you in that situation. Talk to people you respect about it. Calmly. Then take some time to think about the advice and thoughts they offered.

Then make up your own mind. If it has to come to that.

There are married women in my AA group who have husbands that drink excessively and it causes trouble in their marriage. You must have someone you can talk to if you are in this type of relationship. Even Alanon can help. The support you will get, if you are honest about everything, will be significant from these people.

Ok, back to Step 11.

With Step 11 my sponsor sent me on a quest.

He expressed it the same way the Big Book proposed it. He just explained it this way.

He said: Ask God to reveal more of Himself to you. God was ok with you putting Him in a box with your 4 characteristics (from Step 2). Now open yourself for Him to show you more about Who and What He is.

I agreed and went about my day. I kind of felt lost because I didn't know what to do other than express this desire to God that I was ready to learn more about Him.

This is what happened:

About a week or so after I had started my Step Eleven, I was approached by a person at one of my meetings. He walked up to me and said: "Hey I just read this book and thought you might be interested in it. It's called Mr. God this is Anna".

I looked at the book briefly and said to the person: "Thanks a lot, but I'm actually working on my Step 11 right now so I don't have time to go over this. But I appreciate that you took the time to show it to me". He left and I thought nothing of it.

Oddly enough, a couple days later *someone else* came up to me and said: "Hey, you should read this book, I just read and it was awesome. It's called Mr. God this Anna". I said: "Isn't that weird, someone just showed that to me a couple days ago but I'm busy working on my Steps so I don't have time right now, maybe later. Thanks for showing it to me".

Then the next day another person came up to me with the same book. "Hey, you should read this book, it's called Mr. God this is Anna"!

It hit me like a ton of bricks, God wasn't knocking, He was banging at my door! I sheepishly thanked the person for offering me the book and I took it home to read.

Maybe I didn't really expect God to show me more about him. After all I was new to this spirituality thing but after this experience, I began to pay a lot more attention.

Basically, the book was about a little girl in England who was homeless and found by a man who was a self-proclaimed atheist by the name of Fynn.

This little nine-year-old girl had the most extraordinary perception of what God was. She talked to Him differently; she spoke *of* Him differently, and defended Him loudly.

Her friend Fynn didn't know what to make of her, but he was fascinated by her logic and strength. She showed him the beauty of things we often take for granted.

One day she showed him a twisted piece of metal that was full of rust. She told him to look closely at the beauty of the rust. Fynn thought she was crazy, but when he looked closely, he saw what she saw. He was amazed at the wondrous beauty in this twisted piece of metal.

Sometime later on she fell off the roof and landed on that piece of metal ending her life. It was a tragedy but her story was spellbinding and very moving.

The end result was that I had a greater understanding of what God was or could be for me. This was the result of my first Step 11.

This is only one portion of Step 11, to ask God to help you learn more about Him. The other portion is to use Him more often. Make Him a part of your day, every day. The benefits of doing this will soon become apparent. One is removing your dependency on alcohol to help you deal (or evade dealing) with difficult situations ahead of you. Yes, ahead of you. That's called life.

Start asking Him for guidance during your day. Ask how to deal with situations that come up during that day. How to get through to people better, how to be of real help in a way that is beyond your own ability. How to hear what people are really saying. Or even to know when to shut up. That's a big one. At least it was for me!

You'll be surprised some of the answers you will find. If you've been waiting for an answer on something, you may hear someone having a conversation discussing a topic and you'll realize that this is the answer you've been looking for.

Or you may find a newspaper article about something that happened and the answer to your question lies within the article. God has given me answers to my questions in all sorts of ways. Some of them kind of bizarre, but that's what has convinced me He has a great sense of humor. He's creative in a funny sort of way. I think He has the heart of a child too.

So have fun with it, learning and doing. You two will get along great!

See you at Step 12!

Step Twelve

Fantastic! You made it to Step 12!

In this guide I'm going to reveal a special technique to this Step that will change the meaning of Step 12 for you from now on. Let's cover the basics of this amazing and life changing step first.

Let's look at the words to this Step.

"Having had a spiritual awakening as the result of these Steps, we tried to carry this message to alcoholics, and practice these principles in all our affairs."

First off, an incredible promise is mentioned at the beginning of this Step. It promises that our spirit has actually has woke up! That the true essence of who and what we are, has come to life. The emptiness within is becoming full of life. We may not feel it yet, but it's there and it's growing!

This is now your direct line, or communication channel to the God of *your* understanding. What has woke up inside you is the true you. Not only that, it is His essence too! You are one with Him. This will be your communication channel from now on.

The body you look at in the mirror is simply the house you live in. The real you, lies within.

Have you ever seen a beautiful house and then discovered the people who lived there were unhappy or even miserable people? Maybe even hateful people? Just because people live inside a beautiful home, that doesn't make them terrific or loving individuals. Sometimes it's quite the opposite.

However I bet you know some wonderful people that live in homes that are very ugly on the outside. If you've been to any slums you may run into some of the most loving or amazing people you will ever meet.

It's the same with the human body. It's really just a house that contains the spirit or essence of the person inside.

So keep in mind that what the Big Book says can really be true. "Outward appearances are not inward reality at all." (page 48)

It's through this essence that you will begin to feel emotions and thoughts in a spiritual way. One of the most powerful emotions I feel is gratitude. Actually, at times it can become almost overwhelming because I feel it in a spiritual way and it goes much deeper than it did before.

There are times where I've been placed in a situation to help people I had never met before. At an AA meeting I simply told my story in a general way (like it directs in the Big Book) and later found that the words I chose that evening were the exact words these people needed to hear. That's why every time I speak I relate my story differently. It just happens that way.

If I'm asked to speak at a meeting, I think about a few things I would like to cover. Then I let it go after a brief prayer surrendering my will. Sometimes I will talk about these topics, sometimes I don't talk about them at all.

However, many times after I speak at a meeting, I have a person approach me to say how a particular part of my story impacted them. How it is closely related to what they were going through and that it was just what they needed to hear. They were ready now to make a start at their own sobriety. Or face whatever obstacle that was in front of them.

To be an instrument of His work is an amazing thing to me. That He would trust me enough to use me in such a powerful way. This leaves me with the spiritual emotion of gratitude. Once you feel what I'm talking about, you'll understand. It's not the same as the mental emotion of gratitude. It's a lot deeper and much more powerful.

It also says in the sentence that your spiritual awakening is **the** result of these Steps. Not **a** result of the Steps. What that means is that it is a *direct result* of your doing these Steps in this fashion that caused your spirit to wake up. To actually come to life.

There are tens of thousands of people who go on spiritual quests to find themselves that can go on for years. Yet you will do this simple process and find what these people spend years trying to find!

So, keep in mind this new life that's been given to you is **the** (direct) result of you doing these Steps in this order and fashion.

The next element of Step 12 is going to look at is the word "tried" to carry this message to alcoholics.

As I mentioned earlier in another Step, the effort is what counts now, not the outcome. The outcome is left up to the God of your understanding. We are to do the work that's put in front of us, and leave the rest up to Him. He is the mustard seed that will grow even amongst rocks. Just like it says in the "Bigger" Book. So, make the effort to help another alcoholic when it presents itself. At a meeting or elsewhere.

Now for the clincher.

It says to practice these principles in all our affairs. By using these principles in our daily affairs, we are effectively doing 12-Step work all day long!

We can open a door for person as an act of kindness. Whether they tell us to screw off or not is none of our business. Our job is to open the door! Remember it's the effort that counts, not the outcome. The rest is left up to Him.

The key to our action is that now that it is loaded with a spirit of love. This love is called Agape love. It is a love that is given freely with no intention or need of reward or recognition. It is pure, unselfish love.

This is not something that you can do out of your own strength or will power. We get it automatically through the 12 Steps. But by starting our day with this Agape Love, our actions will move mountains. Maybe we won't see it, but significant results will occur.

I'm not sure if you heard about this, but a person was awarded the Nobel Peace prize for discovering and proving that the wings of a butterfly affected the environments on the other side of the world. Imagine that, the wings of a butterfly affecting the world thousands of miles away.

Your words and spiritual acts of kindness will send ripples through the world in the same way but with far more Power behind them. Just keep it simple and do the work He puts in front of you each day. He will provide what you need (and don't be afraid to remind Him) when you need it.

So now you can spend your day constantly doing 12th Step work! It's a truly magical way to spend your day and the rewards will knock your socks off!

I am full of gratitude for the ability to share this with you and reveal the wonder behind these amazing 12 Steps.

All I ask is, when the opportunity arrives, pass it on! Help another by giving them hope. Hope spells out:

H How

O other

P people

E escaped

Best wishes to you my friend

Anonymous Guest

If this guide has helped you, please let others know by leaving a short review on Amazon. It would be appreciated and will help others.

My Other Books

How to Be An Effective Sponsor in AA

Are You a Problem Drinker or an Alcoholic

Recommended Books

The Big Book of Alcoholics Anonymous

The 12 Traditions

A New Pair of Glasses: by Chuck C.

Mr. God This is Anna

I am presently working on doing a video course of this guide on Udemy.com.

Many people have problems reading when they first come to AA, I certainly did. So I am adding this video course as a method to try and help those who have problems reading. Feel free to let others know about the video course once it is completed.

It is also my goal to make an audio version available as well.

God bless.

Printed in Great Britain
by Amazon